ACTING FILM

MAX ZON

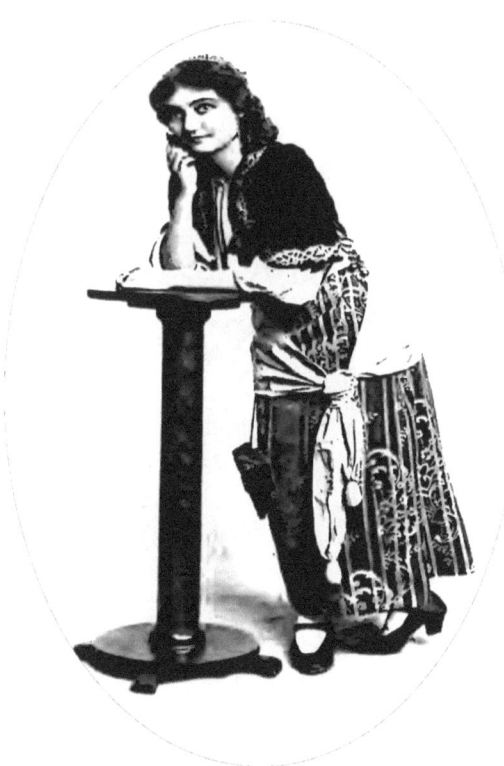

Dtp
and
graphic design

Iacob Adrian

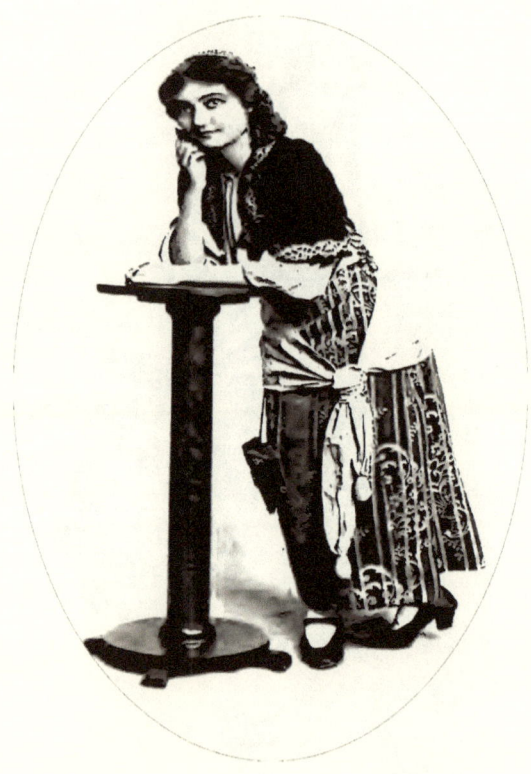

ISBN-13 : 978-1480193048
ISBN-10 : 1480193046

CONTENTS

I. EARLY BEGINNINGS OF THE MOTION PICTURE INDUSTRY   1

II. THE ART OF FILM ACTING   6

III. QUALIFICATIONS   **11**

Talent   11

Health   12

Mental Ability   13

Personal Appearance   14

Personality   15

Age   15

Patience, Pluck and Perseverance Plus Ambition   16

IV. TRAINING   **18**

Physical Culture   18

Breathing   20

Facial Expression and Pantomime Practice   21

Observation   23

Bibliographic sources   26

PART I

EARLY BEGINNINGS OF THE MOTION PICTURE INDUSTRY

IF YOUR grandmother, when a little girl, had been told that perhaps she "would live to see the day" when there would be real moving pictures, she would have been all excitement and like most women and men, too, to be fair to all she would have been filled with that often-tragic possession known as sheet curiosity. Naturally, her first question would have been "What are moving pictures ?" She no doubt had a vague idea of moving or animated pictures. Perhaps, like children of today, she had made her own "movies" by holding an ordinary picture close to the eyes, staring at it a moment in a "cross-eyed" fashion, thus producing the illusion of animation. Staring at a picket fence, striped materials, etc., without blinking the eyes, soon deludes one into believing that the rails, stripes or perpendicular lines are swaying from side to side, while in reality it is only an illusion of the optical organs. Perhaps, also, "grandmother's big brother" had a magic lantern, a toy which like the camera or larger projecting lantern has been likewise improved, so that children of today are also the delighted possessors of toy motion picture machines.

She knew all this, and had no doubt seen stereopticon slides. How could there be anything greater ? And yet the world was destined to know and see something even greater in this line, and if the vast strides made by men of photographic genius can be taken as a criterion for the future, the half has not yet been accomplished.

The earliest beginnings of what might be called moving pictures, though in the crudest form, of course, were about 1872, we are told just a few years after that great civil catastrophe which impeded the progress of discovery and invention in our country and also in foreign lands, since the eyes of the Old World were centered on the efforts of every true American to save his nation according to his own convictions of how that should be done. Although it is known that prior to this date, even before the war, similar experiments were made by various inventors, yet we have little record of the results of these efforts, and nothing noteworthy was accomplished.

About this time (1872), an enterprising Englishman, a resident of America, however, conceived the idea of making motion pictures by the use of successive snap shots. It was his belief that the results could be accomplished by placing several cameras in a row and as the object to be photographed passed, each camera took a "snap." This method was used to photograph the actions of animals in motion, and its greatest success was at the race track. Here, strings attached to each camera were stretched across the track at such a height as to make it impossible for the horse to pass without breaking the string. In so doing the horse really took a snap shot of his action at that moment.

These "snaps," after development, were pieced together and shown on the screen in much the same way that stereopticon slides are exhibited. While he truly accomplished something in the way of animated pictures, and at least set the pace for others to follow, giving the impetus strongly responsible for present day results in animated photography, it is quite apparent that his method could be put to very limited use. In fact, the only experiments he made were the running and walking actions and athletic feats of men and animals as they passed before the row of cameras. It is also obvious that the films thus produced most uninteresting and boring in comparison with those now shown must have depicted very disconnected and jerky movements when thrown on the screen. When we compare this method with that in use to-day and try to consider how it would have been possible for its originator to make pictures of such length as are now shown, we get a clear idea of its impracticability and also a hazy conception of the enormous expense it would involve. Imagine using a separate camera to photograph every action in a picture today ! It would be limited, of course, to progressive actions across the screen, but even so, to merely show some of the racing scenes, etc., which it is our privilege to enjoy, would have necessitated the use of hundreds, nay, thousands of cameras. What an undertaking it would have been!

However, every little bit accomplished in any work brings the dreams of ingenious minds closer to the goal of perfection, and while these experiments revealed no very profitable results at that time, the stimulus which this one man's efforts gave to others was wonderful. Men all over the world immediately set to work for one single accomplishment perfection in motion picture photography.

Each sought to outdo the efforts of others; each one, no doubt, had dreams of giving the world the invention which should mark perfection in animated pictures. Perhaps the greatest of these early efforts was the invention of the "Wizard of Electricity," Thomas A. Edison. This one of his many wonderful inventions, exhibited to the world in 1893, was known as the "Kinetoscope" not in its present state of perfection, but more in the nature of a grown-up toy. It was operated by dropping a coin into the slot, and when thus "fed" it gave to the spectator whose eye was placed to the peephole a momentary glimpse of what appeared to him then to be not only marvelous but almost impossible.

The automatic actions of the photographs in the machine made the figures thereon seem almost alive. Ma'ny doubters refused to believe and declared themselves duped. Though it was impossible that human hands could be working the machine, they still discredited its wonders. Others could only rub their eyes in astonishment and admiration.

Mr. Edison, however, seemed to have little faith in his device except as a coin-eating toy, and neglected to patent his invention in Great Britain.

Thus, visitors to America, with a hazy idea of its far-reaching possibilities, sought to have the machine copied in England. There, one Robert A. Paul, to whom they confided their plans, after investigation learned of Mr. Edison's neglect and thus found it easy to control the machine in that country.

He planned to extend its wonders by perfecting, from the foundation thus laid by Edison, a machine which would throw these animated pictures on the screen. His efforts in this direction met with ultimate success and an amusing incident is told of his first remarkable accomplishment. It is said that in the wee sma' hours, one morning in 1895, he and his associates were rewarded with success by seeing the results of their efforts in the form of the first perfect motion pictures that had been thrown on the screen. Incidentally, this picture was less than fifty feet in length; to-day few are made containing less than five hundred or a thousand feet. But it was such a remarkable achievement and Robert A. Paul had worked so hard for this accomplishment that he and his associates could not refrain from expressing their appreciation of their own work to such an extent that the neighborhood of their little studio was much disturbed in its restful morning slumbers.

So great was the exultation that the blue-coated guardians of peace (or perhaps they did not wear this regalia at that time) were summoned to investigate. When they, too, were allowed to view the remarkable exhibition of real moving pictures, they undoubtedly forgot the complaints of the awakened slumberers, and themselves joined in the shouts of delight, leaving the disturbed citizens in the neighborhood to give way to their wrath by lengthy and not too carefully worded discourses against the prowlers of the night who denied the laborer his just deserts as an occasional inhabitant of dreamland!

However, after this climax of success Robert A. Paul succeeded in producing several other pictures, truly remarkable at this stage of the art, and an English manager, ever on the alert for a novelty which would attract the public and in turn rain gold into his private coffers, negotiated with him for the right to use the machine and pictures in his theater.

Though dubious as to the outcome of the device when "tried out" on a critical public, Paul finally consented to share in the venture. Needless to say, enormous success was the result. Thus began the first of the apparently infinite chain of motion picture theaters. To-day Greater New York City alone contains more than six hundred of these places of amusement some most elaborate, others mere "holes in the wall" with a screen at one end, an operating box at the other, and spectators' benches between. This number is being increased daily, while throughout the whole world, even in the smallest cities and towns, moving picture theaters are being opened constantly and a great many of the large legitimate houses have been turned over to this form of amusement, thus proving its evergrowing popularity.

During these years others in different countries France, Germany and our own United States particularly were making similar experiments, with the result that many different devices were put on the market. However, the invention of Thomas A. Edison, the genius, while greatly improved, not only by himself but by many other remarkable inventors, may be said to have formed the basis of all later machines. The various motion picture devices which flash amusement and instruction for the masses to-day are but improvements on and additions to the wonderful apparatus which startled the whole world during the years 1893-1897.

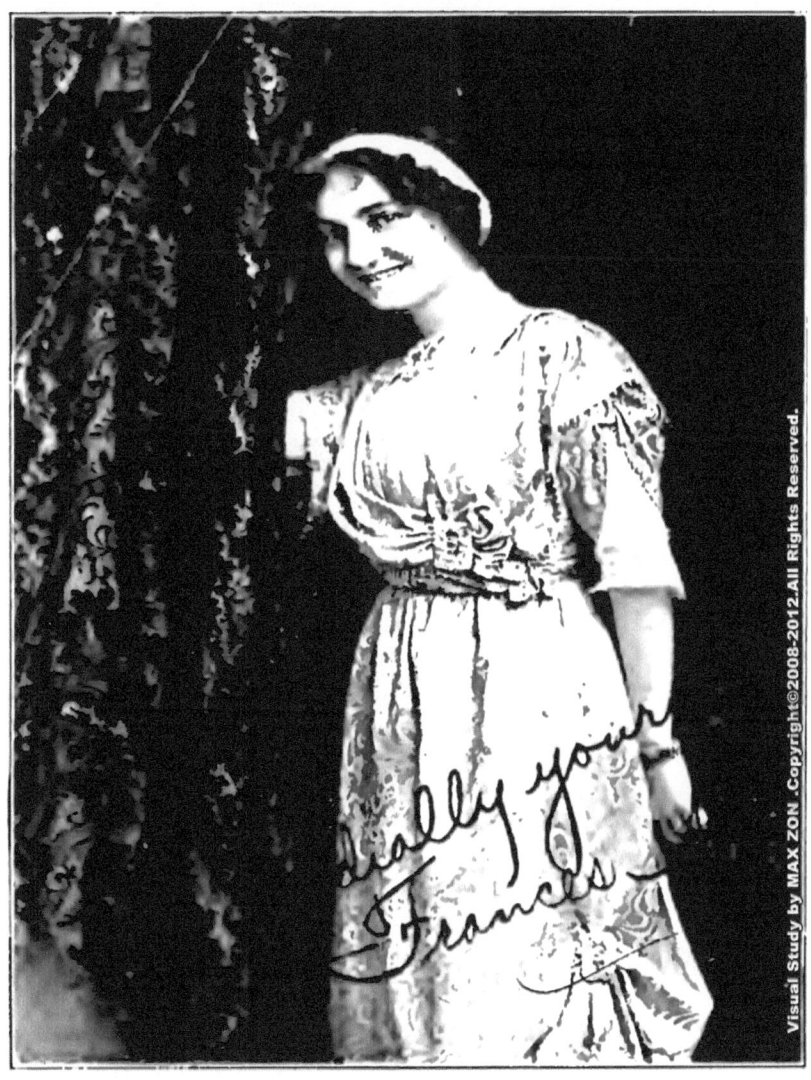

MISS FRANCES AGNEW.
Author, Actress and Photoplayer.

PART II

THE ART OF FILM ACTING

Utterly apart from and at the same time vitally related to the subject of moving pictures, their growth and future possibilities from a scientific standpoint, is the art of film acting. This profession, too, may be said to be in its infancy.

In the beginning only the lesser players could be induced to enter such work. It was far beneath the dignity of an artist! To give them the benefit of the doubt, the salaries at that time were very small, and this may have influenced the better class of actors against the thoughts of becoming motion picture artists. Nevertheless, those who were led into the work were condemned by regular theatrical managers who refused to consider them for parts on the stage after such experience. These moguls denounced the work as tending to make mechanical figures rather than natural actors; they claimed that pantomime without the effect of voice work made the player like a tree, all limbs, to put it frankly, rather than an artist in full control of every muscle and mentality necessary for the production of a real actor. As a result of this attitude toward the work, many of the "movie" players were recruited from the amateur ranks even in those days, and it is estimated that a large percentage of the screen stars of this age had no other experience, but were the most timid of amateurs when they began to pose for the pictures.

As pictures gained in popularity and larger and more elaborate theaters were built in which to entertain the masses with this form of amusement and instruction, the film companies naturally derived a greater profit from the fact that the added number of theaters necessitated an additional number of copies of each picture. This steady growth naturally spurred the makers to better productions ; they sought to place before the public pictures of the highest standard then known. By judicious advertising and just remuneration they secured the best of outside ideas and plots for the foundation of their pictures, thus beginning another interesting and lucrative profession in connection with this work that of scenario writing. These plots were for productions requiring larger casts of players than they had hitherto used, and the makers, recognizing the fact that the better the players, the better the acting, and the more readily could they express almost all the emotions and ideas that can be conveyed even in stage work with the vital assistance of the voice, offered splendid financial inducements to both talented amateurs and capable professionals.

As a result, the artists in the larger theaters, some of them without engagements, others with shaky contracts, used their common sense and decided that "A bird in the hand is worth two in the bush," a "sure thing" at a good salary would more than overbalance the thought that one's standard would be lowered in becoming a "movie" player. Ambitious amateurs, too, plunged into the work with zeal and enthusiasm the remuneration for one and all being a certain amount for each day's work.

This was similar to what is known as "jobbing" that is, working only when needed and being paid for the time in service. After a while, however, the companies began to note and gather data as to the impressions made on the spectators by the personality and work of different players. Their names were not given to the public in any way, but the audiences learned to know their faces and to follow the work of their favorites in the different pictures in which they appeared.

Naturally, this interest and admiration for certain players produced a corresponding admiration and desire to see the films made by their management, and, recognizing this as a good means of advertising, the manufacturers placed these special players on a guaranteed salary basis the number thus engaged forming the regular "stock" organization whose services are at the exclusive command of one company.

The universal popularity and fame gained by actors, if gifted for the work and endowed with an appealing personality, is amazing. Even some of the lesser screen lights are to-day better known throughout the country than a number of the most finished stage stars. They have their admirers in every part of the globe. They assist in making many pictures in the studio or surrounding country, and in a short time these pictures have traveled far and wide and entertained the masses.

"One man in his time plays many parts," is an old saying, but a actor "goes this one better."

He plays many parts in many places on the self- same night. He cannot be in more than one place at a time personally, yet his acting is enjoyed by thousands in many different localities at the same moment. All this has been made possible by the motion picture machine, which is truly one of the wonders of the world ! The "movie" actor does not know his audience, but his audience knows him, and, with a view to gratifying the desire on the part of spectators to know their favorites better (naturally prompted by the personal profit in sight, too), most of the current magazines recognized the wisdom of a department for motion pictures, photo-players, etc., while many other newer magazines are published solely in their interest, with question columns which enable a closer friendship, so to speak, between the delighted spectator and his screen favorite.

Besides this, it is the privilege of many of the screen stars to go and see their audiences personally not only "from the front" where they can sit as one of them, seeing but unseen, and gathering a deal of information as to the varied opinions of their acting while it is being shown on the screen but also from the stage, as oftentimes, especially in the last year, a "movie" favorite is invited to come in person to a theater in the vicinity in which they may be located, to be seen "in the flesh," and speak a word to the audience regarding the motion pictures, also giving laughable accounts of interesting happenings while working in the pictures.

To see a well-known player taking a prominent part in a first-run film and then see and hear the player personally is a treat to the fortunate audiences, and naturally, when it is advertised that Mr. or Miss Blank of the Blank Film Company will appear on the evening of such-and-such a date, the box office receipts show the spectators' appreciation of the pleasure accorded by the manager, thus making it a profitable deal for him. Though a very few players have been known to give their services in such cases for the glory and free advertising it brought, yet the majority of them are independent of this course and only make such appearances for a stipulated remuneration these appearances subject to the consent of the management of the film company by whom they are employed. The amount received ranges from $10.00, $15.00 and $25.00 upward for each appearance, according to the size of the theater (an amount not to be scorned when it is remembered that this is clear profit "on the side"). Some of the more prominent players have added as much as $100.00 to their regular weekly salary as the result of such personal appearances in the motion picture theaters.

There are also opportunities when the management of the company allows a player to accept a vaudeville offer made by some booking agent or theater manager who wishes to feature the motion picture player on a special vaudeville bill. These appearances are made in all the larger cities at various times and net the "movie" star a very large salary, since his fame in the pictures acts as a big advertisement and drawing card in the theater for which he is billed. Thus the deal is a mutual success. Mr. John Bunny, for instance, draws a salary of $1,000.00 a week for occasional weekly engagements in vaudeville. Others of less fame and entertaining ability receive in proportion according to the "goods they have to offer" in the way of a novel vaudeville act and their power as a box office magnet.

Such personal appearances break the monotony of regular picture work and give the actor that which is lacking in the studio applause! It is not always conceit which incites players to long for this indication of public appreciation; more often it is a yearning for encouragement and a desire to know that his efforts to "make good" have not been in vain. "Applause is the spur of noble minds, the end and aim of weak ones."

It is not every city or town, of course, that has the privilege of seeing and hearing the players personally in this way. In places where a stock company is located to take pictures it is not so difficult for the theater manager to make such arrangements, but other cities or towns not among the list possessing the desired scenery for special films cannot enjoy this privilege except in cases where a player goes on a tour to lecture on the subject of motion pictures, or accepts special vaudeville offers, or secures leave of absence from the film company for the purpose of making an extended vaudeville tour throughout the country.

It is amusing to watch the efforts of a actor to extricate himself from the throng of admirers who storm the theater and wait outside for Mr. or Miss Blank, and when at last in sight, even a smile or friendly word is highly cherished because it came from that player. This is only another of the heights of popularity all over the country which this work affords.

As the general public has watched the growth and in a measure become familiar with the origin and expansion of the profession of acting for both men and women, "stage-struck" humanity the world over has in many cases changed its adoration from the legitimate theaters to the motion picture houses. Others who have little interest in regular dramas, comedies, etc., as shown in the legitimate theaters or "opery house," have become intensely interested in motion picture work. Thus "the lure of the screen," we may call it, rather than the lure of the footlights, is becoming stronger than many can resist, and again and again do we hear the question "How can I get a chance?" or, in stage parlance, "break in."

By way of explanation, in passing it is well to note that the word "legitimate" in theatrical parlance is the term used to denote the ordinary speaking stage or dramatic and musical branch of the profession, as contrasted with the variety or vaudeville stage, or the latest branch motion picture acting. Thus we say of a dramatic or musical actor on the speaking stage, "He's in the 'legit/ " which is a professional slang phrase meaning that he is on the legitimate stage ; "He's doing the two-a-day" means that he is in vaudeville, and "He's working in the movies" means that he is posing or playing in motion pictures.

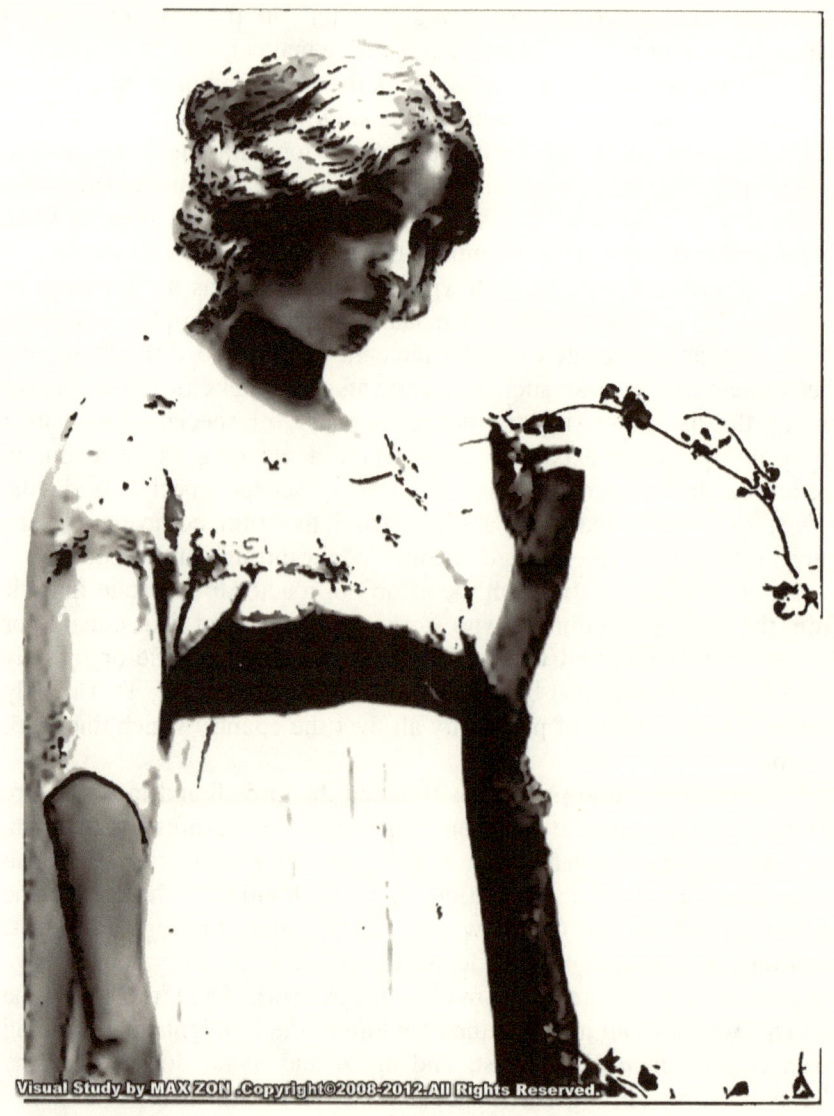

MISS ALICE JOYCE, THE FAMOUS LEADING LADY OF THE KALEM CO.

PART III

QUALIFICATIONS

At this point the "stage-struck" one, with due personal justice, should ask himself, "Am I eligible, or gifted with the qualifications essential to success as a actor ?"

I. TALENT

First and foremost, perhaps, are a natural talent and love for acting and the yearning desire to "make believe you're somebody else," as children say.

It is rare indeed to find an instance in which a normal individual has not at some time in his life experienced what is known as the "stage-struck" fever. It usually attacks young manhood or womanhood between the ages of 15 and 20, though some have had the malady even earlier, others later. A deep-rooted case results in real sane ambition, which nothing can daunt. In a mild form the "fever" soon breaks and other interests in life take its place. No case is to be regarded seriously by those who would check it until it has had control of the "patient" for a year or two. During this time, if really in earnest, he or she will have prepared or planned a fortification against every obstacle and made a firm resolution to succeed, in spite of the draw-backs of financial disability, parental objection or lack of opportunity, even though it might mean longer years of work and waiting. This is the test of true ambition, and when it so asserts itself those interested can do no better than to quell their objections, if any, and substitute helpful encouragement.

To return to the subject of talent, however : this is a most necessary qualification, of course, but it pales into insignificance in comparison with some of the other necessary attributes. Do not understand that one can succeed without talent to a degree, but it has been proven in many cases that even remarkable histrionic ability is not in itself adequate. Talent, with the added force and wise direction of other qualifications, spurred on by patient ambition, cannot fail to win success.

II. HEALTH

Even marked talent can accomplish little without good health, which is an important attribute to success in any undertaking. A weak body is a drawback to any ambition, and especially is it a bar to one who would work for the amusement of the world. In the studio and outdoors the actor is subject to various changes of weather conditions, long hours of steady work and confinement, and discomforts both in traveling and in stationary engagements, which a weakling cannot combat. He may brave the hardships of such a career for a while, but unless strong, physically, a nervous breakdown is inevitable. The actor, more than any other, perhaps, should be almost immune to illness. In legitimate work he may have an understudy to take his place. However, every part is not understudied, especially the stellar roles, and if the actor in the part cannot go on it often necessitates canceling the performance, causing financial loss to each and every member of the company as well as to the management. In the studio it is the same. Perhaps a player is working in a picture which has been continued from the day before. He is expected at the studio at a certain hour and everything is in readiness for work. Should illness prevent his reporting, the director cannot even resort to the understudy system. If the picture had not been started, he could put another player in the part, but it is impossible, under ordinary circumstances, to use two players for the same part in one picture.

The director can do nothing but postpone the picture until the actor's recovery, or re-take the previous scenes with another in the role.

No one can do better than to strengthen himself, physically, by a regular system of freehand or gymnastic exercises. This subject, however, is discussed more fully under the head of training. First of all, attain good health. Examine yourself carefully in this particular. Are you normal in every way? lips red, eyes clear, flesh firm, appetite good, nerves steady? If not, why not? Your mode of living affects your health. Many can trace bad health to certain habits or extravagant methods of living which they insist on retaining, though the advice of their physician is but a repetition of personal knowledge which they could follow themselves if they but had the courage and self-control.

III. MENTAL ABILITY

It has often been said, maliciously, that actors neither need nor possess brains, but are as so much human clay in the hands of the directors. This is a gross insult to the entire profession of acting, no matter in what branch. The mental power of a large percentage of the world's Thespians is not only far above the average, but in many cases remarkable. Genius has been employed in the creation of some of the wonderful characters which have been unfolded to us both on the stage and on the screen. Originality and depth in a characterization are the products of mental force as well as feeling, and no true artist is lacking in that capacity. He who succeeds must be normal mentally. Not all players are marvels of intellect, 'tis true, but in this work, as in all lines of endeavor, talent amounts to little unless its "side partner" is good common-sense. A wonderful education is not necessary. In some cases it is an impossibility in others a waste of money. No circumstances, however, make it necessary for any one to be ignorant. "Accuse not nature, she has done her part : do thou but thine," is sound advice which should be followed. You may recall the announcement some time ago of President Eliot of Harvard niversity, in which he stated that he had selected the contents of an eight-foot book shelf which contained a good and sufficient education any one could personally give to himself if he so desired. This is but another way of saying that systematic home study and sensible reading give in themselves a broad education and enable one to readily think and converse on interesting topics of the day. This is particularly helpful in theatrical work. In the studio one meets a great many different people, and unless he is intellectually on a plane at least with these people he will find himself somewhat alone and isolated.

Then, too, a fair education, coupled with good common sense, THE essential point, carries with it a certain amount of business ability which is a coveted asset and a most beneficial possession in the field of art and literature. It is a deplorable fact, but nevertheless true, that few players have a natural or trained commercial intelligence. They spend their earnings freely, often make ill-advised investments and forget to lay by for the "rainy" season between engagements. The actor is less apt to experience this "rainy" season, since his work goes on all the year 52 weeks but, until he has made a name and created a demand for his services, even he is not exempt from such a time when that most independent of possessions a bank account, however small its beginning serves as a "mighty good comforter." Therefore, beware!
Covet not wealth, but strive for independence!

IV. PERSONAL APPEARANCE

A very important detail, of course, is personal appearance. This is more essential to the actor than to the legitimate actor, since the former cannot resort to the same artifices of make-up which assist and solve many problems for his brother behind the footlights. The camera is most accurate, and to become a good successful actor one must possess at least ordinary regular features and normal physical development. This applies to a straight player, not including the eccentric unusual types which find opportunity in special pictures written expressly for such figures.

Generally speaking, large facial features make a much better impression both in stage and screen work. This does not mean abnormally large, but rather more than mere doll features. Small features can be made to appear larger, but those on whom Nature has bestowed this asset will find it an advantage. It is quite apparent that large features have more strength or carrying power.

Their expressions can be clearly read even in the farthest corner of any room where the changing moods of small doll-like features would hardly be discernible. Large dark expressive eyes are a special asset. In fact, the "windows of the soul" are the strongest medium of expression within the control of the actor.

Both blondes and brunettes, fair and dark complexions, are engaged in picture playing, but the latter are given the preference since it has been found through experience that except in rare cases the brunette photographs better for the screen. A normally healthy person possesses the physical development of his age, height, etc. No more is required, though it is obvious that physical exercise would enhance and strengthen this development.

Closely akin to the subject of personal appearance in general is the question of beauty, which may well be called a coveted possession, but a dangerous weapon in the hands of those endowed with no other qualities. Attractive features are an asset, of course, but do not be obsessed with the idea that beauty is essential or necessary. There are few young men who cannot be said to present a good appearance and few young women who are not pretty to a degree, but on the other hand there are very, very few who can boast of remarkable natural beauty. If so, there would be little need for the manifold "Beauty Secrets" articles which appear in the columns of every daily newspaper.

Cosmetics would be little in demand and there would be no opportunity for the richly paid beauty specialist.

Be neat and magnetic attractive, not gaudy in your dress and demeanor, developing the other gifts bestowed by nature, and you will have little cause to mourn over your lack of exterior beauty or to bewail the fate that did not make you one of the chosen "very, very few."

V. PERSONALITY

This qualification is the embodiment of talent, health, mental and commercial ability and personal appearance. It is an almost indefinable "something" which lures or repels. When it attracts it might be called "charm" and in this meaning it is a wonderful asset in stageland or screenland. Without ambition and average mentality one hasn't the bubbling enthusiasm of an alluring personality. It is personality which wins popularity. Recall the names of your "screen" favorites. Was it some wonderful bit of acting which coerced your admiration ? No ! Wasn't it some manly traits or actions peculiar to himself, or the dainty ways or alluring smile which only she could possess? That is personality magnetism, a quality which every player
seeks to develop to the utmost.

VI. AGE

No fixed rule could be made governing the age of the beginner in screenland. The profession today includes those of all ages from the cradle to 60 or more. This depends almost entirely upon the individual. Every type and age of humanity is at some time or other pictured in the films babies, little children, youth, young manhood or young womanhood, middle age, and life in elderly years. So one must be guided by circumstances.

Under favorable conditions, financially or otherwise, from 15 to 25 is the age when ambition is at its height, and all attention is centered on the accomplishment of one interest, one ideal. However, circumstances alter situations, and many worthy ambitions have been checked and delayed by counteracting influences, but finally the opportunity has come, found a welcome hand and led to success.

Many of the better actors, especially those portraying special character parts, such as old maids and bachelors, and elderly types of different moods, started their careers after the age of 30, many of them having had no experience whatever.

VII. PATIENCE, PLUCK AND PERSEVERANCE, PLUS AMBITION

Extra good doses of the three P's patience, pluck and perseverance must be added to these qualifications, and topping it all one must possess a strong determined ambition which knows no discouragements. In anything you undertake whether it be to become a successful actor or to enter any other profession let the star of hope be an instigator to the "keep on a-tryin' " habit, and when dark clouds of disappointment interpose 'twixt you and that star, when ambition seems in vain and you think "Oh, what's the use," tighten the screw to your courage, apply a little physical "punch" to your efforts and start again.

Cling to hope! When it is lost your ambition begins to melt and failure is the inevitable result.

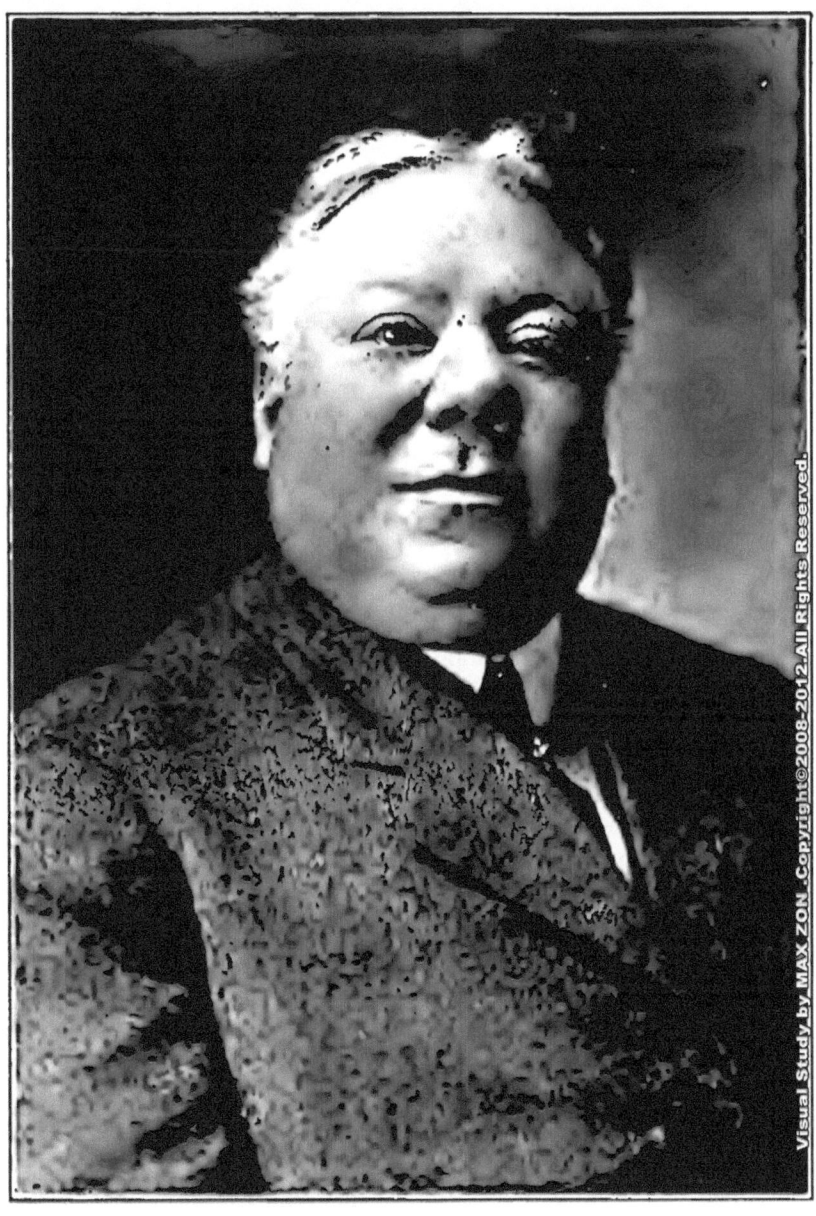

MR. JOHN BUNNY, THE GREAT STAR OF THE GREAT VITAGRAPH CO.

PART IV

TRAINING

Having sounded the subject of qualifications and convinced yourself that you will make a good soldier, the next step is to enter training. There are some methods of personal study and practice which assist in overcoming the disadvantages and embarrassment usually experienced by an amateur when seeking to lay the foundation for a stage career. One of the most important among these is :

I. PHYSICAL CULTURE

This subject is most important in all work, especially in the field of histrionic art. It not only aids in attaining physical strength and good health, but it results in grace of movement and motion and unconscious and correct attitudes of the body. If you are continually conscious of your hands, your arms, your feet, they will always be "in your way," so to speak. You will be awkward in posing and lacking in that grace and refinement of movement which are characteristic of the finished artist. To acquire this grace and ease in a general way depends entirely upon yourself. You may attend physical culture classes, enter gymnasiums, dance, fence or indulge in various outdoor sports such as tennis, golf, rowing, etc., but unless followed diligently your efforts are of little avail. Every one, no doubt, has taken free-hand exercises as a part of the curriculum of school work, but few regard these simple little exercises of any importance. Too much cannot be said of the value of such a system of physical training. Exercises which involve stretching and bending the arms and legs, relaxing the wrist, swaying the body and bending the trunk are all of infinite benefit in strengthening and developing a weak physique, and of just as vital importance in acquiring graceful movements and positions.

Practice suggestions: Such simple exercises as turning the head from side to side and bending it forward and backward; rotating the shoulders, throwing them backward and forward, tend to develop the chest and strengthen the lungs. Swinging and raising the arms, bending at the elbows, thrusting forward, rolling the hand at the wrist and shaking the fingers vigorously, cannot fail to give to these muscles the freedom and relaxation which are so necessary in making expressive gestures. Bending left, right, forward and backward at the waist, swaying the body in all directions (allowing the arms free will in these exercises) relaxes the whole body, strengthens the back and induces correct standing and sitting postures. Raising the leg forward, bent at the knee, and thrusting backward (straightening the leg on this movement and holding the body firmly erect) is one of the simplest and at the same time most helpful exercises to be practiced. It strengthens and gives control over the muscles of the lower limbs and aids in acquiring grace in walking the stage or in private life.

From these general exercises is evolved an infinite number of special exercises, all tending to accomplish the same results. It is not so much the exercise itself, however, as the force and diligence with which it is taken not once, but many times every day. With a feeling that such simple exercise amounts to nothing and is but a waste of time, ambition soon loses itself and grows lax with this part of its development. Hence it is strongly urged that the prospective actor start his system of, training for the work with the determination to give himself a careful physical education, even if it becomes necessary to make his daily practice of at least half an hour as strong a habit as his daily meals. Early morning, just after rising, is the best time for this practice. For the majority, however, this is inconvenient ; but surely some time in the day will furnish a half hour's leisure. Even if you attend a gymnasium with all its benefits, do not neglect these free-hand practice exercises. Not only is this the first step in a thorough training for the stage, but its results are most essential for success in every walk of life.

Dancing and fencing do much to acquire grace and ease of manner, and especially is a knowledge of the former of vital importance in histrionic work. However, they are in themselves but other forms of physical training, and until the opportunity for such study is placed well within one's reach the time should be utilized in free-hand practice which involves no expense whatever. Many of the best known artists on the screen today know nothing of fencing in fact, never handled a sword, unless it may have been in the portrayal of some role requiring the use of this property and also can do naught but social dancing. Yet they are not lacking in that essential to success a graceful stage presence.

The result of this physical practice, if followed systematically, is oftentimes little short of magical.

Awkward mannerisms are enveloped in graceful expressive actions through which is discerned what has no doubt been a dormant personality. Physical self-control paves the way for the assertion of this personality. Mentality responds, and the two forces express the emotions and feelings of a given situation. This is the sum total of acting.

II. BREATHING

Why touch on such a subject in connection with acting ? one might ask. It is true that voice culture is not important in this work, but it is equally true that strong well-developed lungs are essential to good health, and good health is one of the most important qualifications for success in any line of endeavor perhaps the most important.

So, in passing, it is not amiss to urge the importance of vocal and breathing exercises as a vital part of the study. Regular breathing practice is a habit to be encouraged. In this humdrum world of working-to-win we are apt to neglect this part of our physical machinery. It is true we breathe without thought and effort, but few inhale deeply and exhale correctly.

While practicing, stand with the weight of the body on the balls of the feet with the toes turned outward at an easy angle. Always inhale through the nose, taking sufficient breath to perform all the uses to which nature puts it. Few persons inhale sufficient to keep the blood pure. One of the best general exercises for practice is taken thus :

When standing (or seated, if preferred), head and shoulders well up, back unsupported and spine erect, inhale deeply while mentally counting ten, hold the breath for ten counts, then expel through the lips, again counting ten for the exhaling. Repeat this while taking some simple arm exercises, also exhaling on the vowel sound "ah" pitched on all the tones of the voice consecutively. Exhaling on all the other vowel sounds is equally good practice.

Always practice vocal exercises in a freely ventilated room, preferably before an open window or outdoors in dry weather conditions. The results of your practice will be astounding. The chest and lungs will be developed, the blood purified, catarrhal and throat afflictions materially alleviated, and your health and vitality in every way improved.

Remember also that Thos. A. Edison, the genius, has just perfected what he considers his most wonderful invention the talking moving picture machine. These "talking movies" are now being exhibited. The acting is practically the same as on the legitimate stage, the camera photographing the actions and the talking machine recording the voice simultaneously. It is obvious that the voice, its resonance and adaptability to the record will be the first consideration, and the second, one's type and ability as a actor. Hence those "movie" actors and actresses who have a strong healthy physique and a good clear speaking voice, developed by breathing and vocal exercises, will have an advantage over those who, while possessing the voice perhaps, are lacking in ability.

Every effort to become a better player and round out your art is a step toward the coveted goal of success, though you may not be able to see it in just this way in the beginning of your career.

III. FACIAL EXPRESSION AND PANTOMIME PRACTICE

Facial expression is perhaps the most important part of acting. It is an art within itself.

The scenes and actions alone do not tell the minute details of the story. After all is said and done the eyes are really the focus of one's personality in acting. With the aid of other facial features they can express almost all the emotions and passions felt by a human soul. These expressions cannot be taught or merely assumed. It is not enough to say that the brows contract, eyes glare and lips are pressed together in anger, or the eyes are opened wide with the semblance of a twinkle in the corners and a smile on the lips in surprise with pleasure, or the wide-open eyes stare into space and the lips slightly open to express surprise with fear, or a mournful look in the depths of the eyes, the mouth drooping, denotes grief and despair, or the eyes are dancing and the face is lit with a sunny smile in excited enjoyment or rejoicing. These are merely principles for expressions which have no depth of sincerity unless impelled by intense feeling.

A good method of study and practice (always before a mirror, so as to follow your own progress in clear expression) is thus :

First, think of some simple story or create an original plot for yourself, making the principal character your own type. The story is to be told by the expressions of the face and the attitudes of the body.

Next, jot down the various emotions and sentiments felt by the principal character and analyze within your own mind why. Then picture to yourself mentally the actions which would lead up to this emotion if the plot were actually unfolded on the screen.

This should awaken within you the very feeling, almost, of the character and enable you to portray in practice this principal role throughout the different scenes, imagining the other characters and your stage settings. The value of such pantomimic study and practice cannot be overestimated.

This practice is similar to a most important feature of the prescribed course of study in the leading dramatic schools, both in the legitimate and motion picture departments. It is recognized as an independent training. Of course, it is difficult for one character alone to convey the plot, but some idea of the thought in mind can be gained by the student's expressions, poses and movements, and his ability is judged accordingly.

Below is given a list of the emotions and sentiments which find portrayal in the expressions of the face and the actions and attitudes of the body when the player is in full sympathy with the story and feels the part he is conveying:

Rejoicing	Ecstasy
Enjoyment with excitement	Melancholy
Determination	Dignity
Anger with control	Flippancy
Petulance	Tenderness with pity
Patience	Tenderness with love
Surprise with pleasure	Hopefulness
Surprise with pain	Sympathy
Surprise with fear	Kindness
Excitement with anger	Cruelty
Kindly reproof	Pathos
Angry reproof	Grief
Grandeur	Despair
Pride	Agony
Arrogance	Suspicion
Defiance	Threatening
Begging	Indignation
Courage	Caution
Hatred	Anxiety peevish
Love	Anxiety a mother's
Eagerness	Madness

Taking each of these emotions separately, think of some sentence or lines cloaking that emotion, and the pose then taken should be the result of the feeling awakened by this thought and your sympathy with its meaning.

Notice particularly your facial expression in these attitudes. Many of the emotions above can be clearly expressed by the eyes and other features alone.

Get in sympathy with your subject, practice in this way and you will be amazed at the results and the force and control gained over the art of expression.

IV. OBSERVATION

The school of observation is among the best one can attend. Follow its principles in every part of your daily life. When watching a film, do not merely enjoy its story and the unraveling of its plot, but take from the actors portraying it
lessons which will be of vital assistance to you in your personal training. Note the grace of movement, walking, rising, sitting, bowing, management of trains, etc., handling of objects on the stage, etc. Take an idea or situation from the play and later practice its portrayal yourself, but do not imitate. In imitation one loses individual touches and personality. Strive for originality, practice diligently and remember:

"The more we work, the more we win."

V . Film cast and crew

A illustrious unknown film producer found a story, hire a screenwriter for the script, and after all hires a director who provide the vision of film with the director of photography, and after all this hires the rest of the team and the actors .

The most important persons are : 1.The **PRODUCER** - owner of the film ; 2.The **SCREENWRITER** - owner of the story ; 3.The **DIRECTOR** - owner of the vision

1. Production	1.0 Production **PRODUCER** Executive Producer Line Producer Production Manager Unit Manager Production Coordinator Postproduction Supervisor Production Assistant **SCREENWRITER** Script Supervisor Stunt Coordinator Casting Director	1.1 Directing **DIRECTOR** First Assistant Director Second Assistant Director	1.2 Locations Location Manager Assistant Location Manager Location Scout Location Assistant Location Production Assistant	1.3 Additional production credits Legal Counsel Accountant Insurance Broker System administrator			
2. Art Department	2.0 Production Designer	2.1 Art Art Director Assistant Art Director Illustrator	2.2 Sets and Construction Set Designer Set Decorator Buyer Lead Man Set Dresser Greensman Construction Coordinator Construction Head Carpenter Key Scenic	2.3 Props Props Master Propmaker Weapons master	2.4 Costume Department Costume designer Costume Supervisor Key Costumer Costume Standby Art Finisher Costume Buyer Cutter	2.5 Hair and make-up Make-up Artist Hairdresser	2.6 Special Effects Special Effects Supervisor Special Effects Assistant

24

3. Camera	Cinematographer Director of Photography	Camera Operator First Assistant Camera Second Assistant Camera	Camera Film Loader Camera Production Assistant	Digital Imaging Technician Steadicam Operator	Motion Control Technician		
4. Production Sound	Production Sound Engineer	Production Sound Mixer	Boom Operator	Utility Sound Technician			
5. Grip	Key grip	Best boy (Grip)	Dolly grip	Grips			
6. Electrical	Gaffer	Best boy (Electrical)	Lighting Technician				
7. Post-production	7.1 Editorial	Film Editor	Negative Cutter	Colorist	Telecine Colorist		
	7.2 Visual Effects Visual Effects Producer	Visual Effects Creative Director	Visual Effects Supervisor	Visual Effects Editor	Compositor	Rotoscope Artists/ Paint Artists	Matte Painter
	7.3 Sound/Music Sound Designer	Dialogue Editor	Sound Editor	Re-recording Mixer	Music Supervisor	The Composer	Foley Artist
8. Cast	8.1 Actors	Leading actor	Character actor	Supporting actor	Cameos	Extras (actors)	

Bibliographic sources :

Motion picture acting; how to prepare for photoplaying, what qualifications are necessary, how to secure an engagement, salaries paid to photoplayers ([c1913])

Author: Agnew, Frances, b. 1891

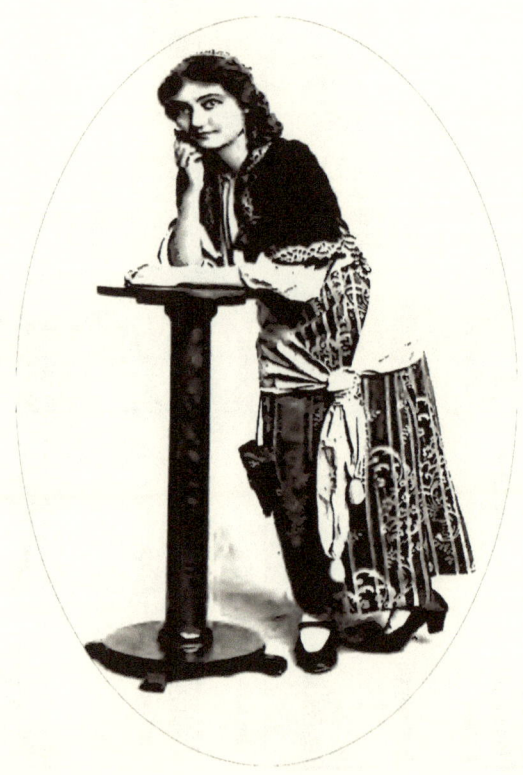

www.ingramcontent.com/pod-product-compliance
Lightning Source LLC
Chambersburg PA
CBHW021854170526
45157CB00006B/2447